Legal & Disclaimer

The information contained in this book has been compiled from sources deemed reliable, and it is accurate to the best of the Author's knowledge. However, the Author cannot guarantee its accuracy and validity so cannot be held liable for any errors or omissions. Changes are periodically made to this book. You must consult your doctor or get professional medical advice before using any of the suggested remedies, techniques, or information in this book.

Upon using the information contained in this book, you agree to hold harmless the Author from and against any damages, costs and expenses, including any legal fees, potentially resulting from the application of any of the information provided by this guide. This disclaimer applies to any damages or injury caused by the use and application, whether directly or indirectly, of any advice or information presented, whether for breach of contract, tort, negligence, personal injury, criminal intent, or under any other cause of action.

Contents

Acknowledgement

As a full time mom and a dedicated cook of the household, it was important for me that my time was able to be spent with my family and friends.

Jessie, my baby girl, was a reminder of that.

Without her, and my loving husband, Zack, I would not have been inspired to take the first step in the creation of this book to help others spend more time with their family and get things done efficiently.

I would also like to give my thanks to Luther, my brother, for his constant encouragement and assessment of my work, which pushed me further to make this book polished and ready to be shared with the world.

Lastly, I would like to give my most heartfelt thanks to all my readers out there for giving me the chance to show you how efficient and easy the world of Crock-Pot cooking can be and how it can help you save a lot of time and effort.

Introduction

Slow Cooking is a method of food preparation that relies mainly on cooking for a long amount of time with low or gradual heat. It refers to a set-up of "slow cooker" which is focused on recipes involving "one pot" only. They are easy and uncomplicated, and food prep is very minimal. As long as you have a recipe prepared, you can place the ingredients in a heavy pot and leave it. Soon you will have a delicious and delightful dish in front of you.

Congratulations, and thank you for purchasing this book about Crock-Pot cooking. There are so many ways you can use this versatile cookware. Choose from a wide range of recipes in this book where you can find healthy and nutritious meals, meat entrees for those who love eating meat and imagine – you can even prepare desserts and breakfast using the Crock-Pot cooker! Amazing!

So let me now take you to the wonderful world of Crock-Pot cooking. Put on your cooking apron and toque and explore this wonderful cooking method to prepare new and exciting meals for your friends and family!

Happy cooking!

Why I love using the Crock-Pot

Fast food is so ubiquitous in everyone's lifestyle nowadays that it is hard to imagine going through a day without it. With the growing number of varieties that permeate every corner of the city, you will choose it due to its convenience, albeit far from the healthy diet that we are supposed to be getting. Busy people tend to patronize it, because, hey, who has time to prepare meals when you already have a lot on your plate? On the other end of the spectrum, in terms of speed when it comes to cooking, is a healthier and more satisfying option. The Crock-Pot, or slow cooking, has been the go-to of even busy people because of its easy preparation, and the quality of food that it yields is worth the time and the effort.

How can you benefit from this cookbook?

Given the remarkable background of the Crock-Pot, or slow cooking, this cookbook could greatly benefit you if you are single, a working parent, or just too busy to prepare food in general, and you want to serve something that requires minimal effort but is healthy and tastes special. The recipes in this cookbook can help you maximize the use of your Crock-Pot cooker and will get you excited about trying new recipes—from the traditional stew to appetizing entrees, to fish and veggie meals, and even sweet concoctions. Get started with the recipes provided in the succeeding chapters.

Chapter 1 – Choosing the Perfect Crock-Pot Cooker

In the market place there are a lot of Crock-Pots to choose from. But how do you know is the best one that suites your needs? It might be quite confusing since there are a lot of factors that you need to consider before purchasing one for your home cooking. But first what composes the basics of the Crock-Pot.

The Crock-Pot Design

The slow cooker is typically composed of this 4 key parts

The Lid: Traps the moisture in, yet does not overly pressurize the inside of the pot. Since the lid is made of glass, it's very effective in keeping the atmospheric pressure inside for low-heat cooking.

The Crock: The main cooking pot and heat bank which is made of glazed porcelain or ceramic.

The Housing: the heat supplier and where the crock resides. It's made of metal.

The Heat Setting: Normally a knob located on the front of the housing that has low, medium, and high heat. It also sometimes has a "keep warm" setting.

Why purchase a Crock-Pot?

Many of us are wondering why it is necessary to purchase this appliance when we can cook things faster on the stove. Here are just a few reasons that distinguish the Crock-Pot pot from other cookware:

Energy Efficient: They use an equivalent electricity of two light bulbs compared to electrical ovens.

Saves Money: You can use cheaper cuts of meat, since the slow cooking process extracts the flavor, and you can put more veggies.

Fat Trimmer: Due to the long process, the fat content of the meat is already sufficient to make dishes tasty.

Saves Time and Effort: You just need to put the ingredients in, turn it on, and you are good to go! No more long preparation time needed and you don't need to attend to it.

Choosing the right Crock-Pot is chief if you want to have the perfect meal. Just like anything else in life there are varied options. There are several different price ranges, ranges of quality, size capacities, features, and so on. It is important to look at all factors and do your own investigation before committing to a particular Crock-Pot for you or your family.

Key Factors in Choosing a Crock-Pot

Price: Remember that Crock-Pots have different prices for a reason. That should not, however, keep you from enjoying a well-cooked and perfect meal each time.

Quality: Of course we all know the old saying, "you get what you pay for" and this is very true. Typically, there are well-known and proven brands that offer a superior level of lifetime service. Remember, you can purchase a Crock-Pot that may last 2 years and cost a lot less or a higher quality, and hence higher priced, one that may last 20 years.

Size: This will depend on your lifestyle. If it is just you then you could get away with a small Crock-Pot, however a family will require a higher capacity one.

Features: Again, there is the basic Crock-Pot that cooks and keeps the food warm. That is the most basic function. Of course like almost every other product, other versions have options such as advanced timers and other such features.

Versatility: Know what your Crock-Pot can do. There are literally hundreds of recipes and types of meals your Crock-Pot can prepare. So think outside of just basic soups and stews.

Storage: Many of us have small kitchens where counter space is a highly prized piece of real estate. Make sure the right Crock-Pot will fit in your kitchen and is in a place where it is safe when not in use.

All in all, there is much to consider. Know what you want and make sure to be prepared when you decide. A Crock-Pot for whatever your situation is a great investment and something you will use again and again. From one enthusiastic home cook to another: Bon appétit!

Chapter 2 – Breakfast

One of the most important meals of the day is breakfast. It is quite amazing to know that even the Crock-Pot cooker can prepare this type of meal. So if you want to have a hearty breakfast that will fuel you for the rest of the day, go ahead and try these wonderful recipes.

Meatloaf Breakfast

Ingredients

- 1 tablespoon coconut oil
- 2 cups diced onion
- 2 lbs ground pork
- 2 whole eggs
- ½ cup almond flour
- 1 tablespoon powdered garlic
- 2 teaspoons fennel seeds
- 2 teaspoons oregano (dried)
- 2 teaspoons red pepper flakes
- 2 teaspoons sage (ground)
- 2 teaspoons thyme (dried)
- 1 teaspoon black pepper
- 1 teaspoon paprika
- 1 teaspoon sea salt

Directions

1. Heat a tablespoon of coconut oil over low flame and cook onions until it becomes translucent. Remove from flame and set aside.
2. Using a large-sized bowl, add all of the ingredients except ground pork. Stir to combine well.
3. Add the ground pork with the onions in the bowl. Using your hands, mix it all together and make sure that all is combined evenly.

4. Form the meat mixture into a loaf and place it on a Crock-Pot or slow cooker. Cook for about 3 hours on low setting. Let sit for about 15-30 minutes. Then you can remove it from the slow cooker.
5. Transfer to a plate and slice to serving portions. Enjoy!

Breakfast Porridge

Ingredients

- ½ cup wild or red rice
- ½ cup oats (choose the steel-cut ones)
- ¼ cup faro or pearl barley
- ½ cup wheat cereal or farina
- 1 piece of orange peel (cut to 2 inch slices)
- 1 piece of cinnamon stick
- 1-2 tablespoons brown sugar (choose from dark or light color)
- ¼ teaspoon salt
- ¼ cup dried fruit (choose your favorite fruits)
- 5 cups water
- Chopped nuts, milk or maple syrup to serve (optional)

Directions

1. 12 hours before serving, you can prepare this dish in time for breakfast. Place rice, barley, farina and oats inside the slow cooker. Mix in cinnamon stick, salt, sugar, 5 cups water, and orange peel. Also add the dried fruit of your choice.
2. Set the slow cooker for the porridge cycle, so that it will be cooked and prepared once you wake up in the morning. If you don't have a porridge cycle, you can cook for about an hour and warm in the morning.
3. Serve with syrup or milk, top with nuts if you prefer. Enjoy!

Spinach, Ham, and Egg Casserole

Ingredients

- 6 large eggs
- ½ teaspoon salt
- ¼ teaspoon black pepper
- ¼ cup milk
- ½ cup Greek yogurt

- ½ teaspoon thyme
- ½ teaspoon powdered onion
- ½ teaspoon powdered garlic
- 1/3 cup of mushrooms (diced)
- 1 cup baby spinach
- 1 cup shredded cheese (Pepper jack)
- 1 cup diced ham

Directions

1. Using a bowl, combine pepper, salt, eggs, yogurt, milk, thyme, powdered onion, and powdered garlic and whisk together till smooth.
2. Add in mushrooms, cheese, ham and spinach.
3. Spray your slow cooker using a non-stick oil.
4. Put the egg mixture inside and cover.
5. Cook over high for 1 ½ to 2 hours until the eggs set.
6. Slice and serve hot. Enjoy!

Breakfast Casserole

Ingredients

- One bag (32 oz) of hash brown potatoes (frozen)
- 1 lb bacon
- 1 piece of diced small onion
- 8 oz sharp cheddar cheese (shredded)
- ½ of one diced bell pepper (red)
- ½ of one diced bell pepper (green)
- 12 eggs
- 1 cup milk

Directions

1. Slice bacon into small pieces and cook well. Drain excess fat.
2. Add half the bag of hash browns at the bottom of the Crock-Pot, then add half of the cooked bacon, half onions, half of the red and green bell peppers and shredded cheese.
3. Place remaining half-bag of hash browns on top. Followed by the remaining bacon, onions, cheese and the red and green bell peppers.
4. Meanwhile, crack 12 eggs on a bowl and whisk together with the milk. Pour this mixture inside the Crock-Pot and add pepper and salt.
5. Cook the mixture for 4 hours on low. Serve hot and enjoy!

Medjool Dates Breakfast Quinoa

Ingredients

- 1 cup quinoa
- 3 cups milk
- 4 pieces of chopped medjool date
- ¼ cup pepitas
- 1 piece of diced and peeled apple
- 2 teaspoons cinnamon
- ¼ teaspoon nutmeg
- 1 teaspoon vanilla extract
- ¼ teaspoon salt

Directions

1. Place all of the ingredients inside the Crock-Pot.
2. Cover and cook on high for about 2 hours or until liquid is fully absorbed.
3. You can either cook this overnight by setting your Crock-Pot on low for about 8 hours before going to bed. Once you wake up, it should be ready by then.
4. Serve warm and enjoy the day!

* Leftovers can last for about a week inside the refrigerator.

Chapter 4 – Steamy Stews and Delicious Soups

For the cold and chilly weather, the best way to keep warm is by eating a bowl of soup or a hearty stew. It's also a great way to make you feel better, especially when you are sick with a flu. Here, you will find heart-warming recipes that will surely give you comfort and make you feel good.

Pork Stew Delight

Ingredients

- 2 small sized onions (sliced thinly)
- 6 cloves of garlic (smashed and peeled)
- ½ lb of baby carrots
- Kosher salt
- Fresh ground black pepper
- 3 lbs pork shoulders (cut to 1½ inch thick cubes)
- 1 tablespoon of your preferred seasoning blend
- 1 tablespoon fish sauce
- 1 small sized cabbage (cut them to 8 wedges)
- 1 cup of store-bought Paleo marinara sauce
- 1 tablespoon balsamic vinegar
- ¼ cup of Italian parsley (finely chopped)

Directions

1. Slice the onions and smash garlic cloves. Add them inside the slow cooker with the carrots. Season with salt and pepper.
2. Cut the pork meat into cubes. Place it on a bowl and add fish sauce and your preferred seasoning blend. Add a few more pepper and salt. Toss and combine well.

3. Place the pork on top of the carrots and onions. Add the cabbage wedges. Drizzle your marinara sauce on top of the cabbage and season with additional pepper and salt.
4. Cover and cook for about 8-10 hours. Once the veggies and pork are fork tender, adjust seasoning with pepper, salt, and balsamic vinegar.
5. Once done, ladle a small amount on your plate. Sprinkle with Italian parsley. Serve hot and enjoy!

Chocolicious Chicken Mole Stew

Ingredients

- 2 lbs chicken (bone in and skin removed)
- Pepper and salt for tasting & seasoning
- 2 tablespoons ghee
- 1 medium sized onion (chopped)
- 4 cloves of garlic (minced or crushed)
- 6-7 pieces of whole tomatoes (seeded, peeled and chopped)
- 5 pieces of dried chili peppers (New Mexico variant; chopped and rehydrated)
- ¼ cup of almond butter
- 2.5 oz dark chocolate (get the 70% or above)
- 1 teaspoon sea salt
- 1 teaspoon powdered cumin
- ½ teaspoon powdered cinnamon
- ½ teaspoon guajillpo chili powder
- Avocado (chopped)
- Cilantro (chopped)
- Jalapeno (chopped)

Directions

1. Season your chicken with pepper and salt.
2. Place a pan on medium-high heat and add the ghee. Once the ghee is heated through, cook the chicken until golden brown on all sides. Do this in batches to avoid overcrowding the chicken. Once done, place chicken in your slow cooker.
3. Using the same pan, sauté onions and garlic. Cook for about 1-2 minutes or until onions are translucent and garlic is fragrant. Transfer sautéed onion and garlic to the slow cooker.

4. Add chili peppers, tomatoes, dark chocolate, almond butter, spices, and salt to the slow cooker. Cover and cook for about 4-6 hours on low heat. If chicken meat falls apart, it's done.
5. Once cooked, top with cilantro, jalapeno and avocado. Serve and enjoy!

Easy Pea-sy Soup

Ingredients

- ½ cup fresh parsley (chopped; plus add 8-10 parsley stems more)
- 4 sprigs of thyme
- 1 lb green split peas (rinsed and picked over)
- 1 large sized leek (use the light green and white part only; halved and sliced thinly)
- 2 stalks of chopped celery
- 2 pieces of carrots (chopped)
- Salt and pepper
- Smoked leg of turkey (around 1to 1 ½ lbs)
- ¼ cup plain yogurt (non-fat)
- ½ cup frozen peas (thawed)
- Crusty bread to serve (optional)

Directions

1. Tie thyme together with parsley stems using a kitchen string. Place it inside the slow cooker. Add leek, split peas, carrots, celery, a teaspoon of salt and half a teaspoon of pepper. Mix them to combine. Add turkey leg plus 7 cups of water then cover.
2. Cook on low for about 6-8 hours or until peas and turkey are tender. Once done, discard the twigs of herb. Discard bone and skin from the turkey then shred its meat.
3. Stir the soup vigorously to break peas and make soup smoother. You can add water if it is too thick for your preference.
4. Add about ¾ of the shredded turkey into the soup. Set aside some meat for garnishing. Add chopped parsley and season with pepper and salt.
5. Ladle soup into serving bowls. Top with thawed green peas and meat. Serve with bread if you want. Enjoy!

Beans and Sausage Pasta Stew

Ingredients

- 1 piece of onion (sliced to ½ inch pieces)
- 2 carrots (chopped finely)
- 4 cloves of garlic (chopped finely)
- 8 oz white beans (dried; picked over and rinsed)
- 6-8 sprigs of thyme (fresh and tied with kitchen twine)
- 1 lb Italian sausages (hot or sweet flavored; around 4-6 links)
- 1 14 oz can of fire-roasted tomatoes (diced)
- 3 cups stock or chicken broth (use the low-sodium variety)
- 1 4 oz piece of Parmesan chunk rind (optional; plus some grated Parmesan to serve)
- ½ cup pasta
- 2 tablespoons freshly chopped flat-leaf parsley
- 2 teaspoons balsamic vinegar
- Fresh ground pepper and Kosher salt
- Crusty bread to serve

Directions

1. Spread onion at the bottom of the Crock-Pot cooker. Top it with garlic, carrots, white beans, bundle of thyme and the sausage links. Mix in the canned tomatoes together with 3 cups of water and broth inside the Crock-Pot. Add Parmesan rind if you will be using it.
2. Cook on high for about 4-5 hours or 7-8 hours if on low setting. The beans will become tender and start falling apart.
3. Once done, uncover and discard the bundle of thyme and Parmesan rind. Remove sausage links and place on cutting board.
4. Stir in pasta, cover, and continue to cook around 20 minutes or until pasta is cooked.
5. Turn heat off and cut sausages to small pieces then stir in the stew. Add vinegar and parsley. Season with pepper and salt.
6. Ladle into serving bowls and top with grated Parmesan. Serve with bread if desired. Enjoy!

Chapter 5 – Meat Entrees

Of course, slow cooking is best when it comes to meat entrees. Create your own fabulous and delicious meat recipes that will leave your whole family and friends wanting for more. Go ahead and check them out!

Easy Meatballs and Spaghetti Squash

Ingredients

- 1 medium sized squash
- 1 lb. Italian sausage (ground)
- 1 (14 oz.) can of tomato sauce
- 2 tablespoons spicy pepper relish
- 6 cloves of garlic (whole)
- 2 tablespoons olive oil
- Italian seasoning (for tasting)

Directions

1. Prepare a large sized, 6 quarts slow cooker. Put olive oil, pepper relish, tomato sauce, and Italian seasoning inside the cooker. Stir well to combine.
2. Cut the squash and spoon out all of the seeds. Place the squash halves facing down inside the slow cooker.
3. Roll the ground sausage into balls and fit inside the cooker around the squash.
4. Cook for about 3 hours on high heat.
5. Once done, scrape squash using a fork and this will look like spaghetti strands. Place it on a plate and top it with the sauce and meatballs.
6. Garnish on top with parsley. Serve hot and enjoy!

Chicken with Gravy Slow Cooker style

Ingredients

- 4-5 lbs whole chicken
- 2 tablespoons ghee
- 2 medium sized onions (chopped)
- 6 cloves peeled garlic
- 1 teaspoon tomato paste
- ¼ cup chicken stock
- ¼ cup white wine
- Your favorite seasoning
- Kosher salt
- Fresh ground pepper

Directions

1. Prepare and chop all of your vegetables.
2. Using a large-sized cast iron pan, melt ghee over medium to high heat. Sauté the garlic and onions. Add tomato paste. Cook for about 8-10 minutes and season the veggies with pepper and salt.
3. When all the veggies are lightly browned and soft, deglaze pan with white wine and transfer everything in your slow cooker.
4. Meanwhile, season your chicken with pepper and salt and your favorite seasoning. Make sure to season them inside and out. Place the chicken, breast facing down, inside the cooker. Cook on low heat for about 4-6 hours.
5. Once the cooking is done, take the chicken out and let it sit for about 20 minutes.
6. Take the excess fat on top of the vegetables inside the slow cooker. Using an immersion blender or hand blender, blend thoroughly until mixture turned to mouth-watering gravy. Adjust seasoning according to preference.
7. Slice or rip off your chicken using your hands (this is pretty much exciting!). Place on a serving plate and put gravy on top or a small bowl.
8. Eat up and enjoy!

Slow Cooked Chicken Pad Thai on Veggie Noodles

Ingredients

- 2-3 lbs of chicken breast or thigh (remove the skin)
- 2 medium sized zucchini
- 1 large carrot
- 1 handful of bean sprouts (optional)
- 1 bunch of green onions (to be used for garnish and the sauce)
- 1 cup coconut milk
- 1 cup stock (chicken)
- 2 tablespoons sunflower seed butter
- 1 tablespoon Coconut Aminos
- 2 teaspoons fish sauce
- 2 teaspoons powdered ginger
- 1 teaspoon cayenne pepper
- 1 teaspoon red pepper flakes
- Pepper and salt to season the chicken
- Cashews (chopped; to be used for garnishing)
- Cilantro (chopped; also for garnishing)

Directions

1. Season your chicken with pepper, salt, ginger powder, and cayenne pepper. Using the Crock-Pot, add chicken stock and coconut milk. Stir them well.
2. Add sunflower seed butter, fish sauce, coconut aminos, ginger, chopped green onions, garlic, red pepper and cayenne pepper. Mix well until the sunflower seed butter dissolved completely.
3. Put the chicken into the soup base.
4. Meanwhile, turn the zucchini into noodles. Using your paleo spiralizer, place zucchini and spiralize with Blade C. Shred the carrots and wash bean sprouts.
5. Toss the carrots, zucchini noodles, and bean sprouts in a bowl. Mix well.
6. Place the veggie noodles on top of the chicken and liquid base and press down to immerse the veggies lightly. The veggies need to be steamed and not thoroughly cooked or stewed.
7. Cook for about 3½ to 4 hours on low heat. Use a 4-quart thick pan or slow cooker.
8. Do not cook for more than 6 hours. Remove and strain the veggie noodles and make sure that there is not any excess liquid on them.

9. Remove chicken. You can debone it, depending on your preference. Shred or chop chicken into serving strips.
10. Arrange in bowl by placing veggie noodles and adding chicken on top of the noodles. Pour in some broth and garnish with chopped cilantro, green onions, and cashews. Serve hot and enjoy!

Slow Cooker Smoky Brisket

Ingredients

- 2 tablespoons dark brown sugar
- 2 tablespoons smoked paprika
- 2 tablespoons cumin (ground)
- Kosher salt and black pepper (freshly ground)
- 1 5 lbs flat-cut brisket (trim excess fat if needed)
- 6 tablespoons tomato sauce
- 2 tablespoons apple cider vinegar
- 2 tablespoons honey
- 2 tablespoons molasses (unsulfured is preferred)
- 2 cans of chipotles (choose the can in adobo sauce; seed, stem and minced)
- 1 medium-sized sweet onion (sliced to thin half-moons)

Directions

1. Combine sugar, cumin, paprika, 1 ½ teaspoons of salt and a half teaspoon of pepper using a small bowl. Use this to rub the brisket on both sides.
2. Mix the vinegar, tomato sauce, honey, chipotles and molasses until it becomes smooth. Spread over both sides of the brisket.
3. Place the brisket in a 5 or 6-quart Crock-Pot cooker. Make sure that the whole brisket will fit the Crock-Pot cooker. If not, cut the brisket in half. Put the onion of top of the brisket. Cook and cover for about 5-6 hours if cooking on high and 8-9 hours if cooking on low. Once done, transfer brisket with the onion onto a cutting board and let rest.
4. Meanwhile, pour sauce on a fat separator. Set it aside for a couple of minutes. Once done, pour this on a saucepan and simmer over medium to high heat. Stir it occasionally. Cook until it is reduced to half (around 8 minutes).
5. Cut brisket into half-inch-thick slices. Make sure to cut it against its grain. Transfer to a plate and serve with onion on top and sauce. Enjoy!

Pot Roast with Red Wine and Root Veggies

Ingredients

- 3/4 cup orange juice (freshly squeezed and strained for pulps)
- 3 tablespoons garlic (minced)
- 1/4 cup tomato paste (plus another tablespoon)
- 1 teaspoon sage (dried)
- 1 3½ lbs beef chuck roast (choose the boneless type)
- 2 teaspoons kosher salt
- 10 grinds black pepper
- 2 tablespoons butter (unsalted)
- 1½ cups Spanish onion (chopped finely)
- 3/4 cup celery (chopped finely)
- 3/4 cup carrots (peeled and chopped finely)
- 3/4 cup parsnips ((peeled and finely chopped)
- 1/4 cup all-purpose flour
- 1 cup red wine (like Pinot Noir)
- 1 14 oz canned tomatoes (whole and peeled with juice)
- 1/4 cup chicken stock (low-sodium)
- 1 tablespoon honey
- 4 sprigs of rosemary (fresh and tied together using kitchen twine)
- Cooked polenta to serve

Directions

1. Using a wooden spoon, combine 2 tablespoons of garlic, 1/4 cup of orange juice, 1 tablespoon of tomato paste, plus sage. Add meat and coat evenly with this marinade. Season evenly with pepper and salt.
2. Meanwhile, using a heavy pan, heat the butter over medium to high heat. Once melted, add onions, parsnips, celery, carrots, and the remaining tablespoon of garlic. Sauté and stir occasionally until onions are become very soft and veggies are becoming a bit brown for around 10 minutes.
3. Stir the flour with remaining 1/4 cup tomato paste then cook until flour can't be seen for about one minute. Remove pan from the heat then add wine. Return pan to the heat and increase temperature to high. Stir until sauce becomes thick for about 2 minutes. Add tomatoes, stock, honey, remaining half cup of orange juice, and rosemary then boil for about 5 minutes. Gently crush tomatoes using your potato masher and stir sauce.

21

4. Using your Crock-Pot cooker, pour the sauce over beef and cover. Cook on low for about 10 hours. Once done, remove the rosemary and discard. Use a ladle or large spoon to skim fat off the surface of the sauce.

5. Transfer meat on cutting board and cut to chunks. Return to its sauce then prepare by ladling the meat with sauce over a plate of polenta. Serve hot and enjoy!

Chapter 6 – Fish and Vegetarian Meals

The versatility of the Crock-Pot is truly amazing. Imagine that you can even prepare healthy and nutritious food using this cookware. Grab your aprons and keep on cooking!

Salmon Head with Spiralized Noodles

Ingredients

- 1 salmon head with tails and other remaining parts
- 1 small onion (sliced)
- 1 bulb of green garlic (minced)
- 1 cup of wakame
- 1 piece of medium-sized ginger (sliver a few pieces of ginger; peel and mince remaining to get at least a tablespoon)
- ¼ cup of coconut aminos
- ¼ cup of mirin (you can also use coconut vinegar)
- 3 zucchinis (spiralized in Blade C)
- Chilies and chives to be used for garnishing

Directions

1. Put the salmon head and its parts into the slow cooker. Add the slivered ginger, water and cover. Cook over high heat for about 1-2 hours.
2. Strain the broth and separate meat. Once you have strained, place it back on a medium stock pot.
3. Add onion, garlic, minced ginger, mirin, wakame, and tamari. Slowly heat the soup and let simmer. Don't boil. Cook for about 20 minutes.
4. Add the spiralized zucchini and cook for another 10-15 minutes or until the zucchinis are cooked.

5. Ladle the soup into bowls and top with chilies and chives. Serve hot and enjoy!

Slow Cooked Mashed Sweet Potatoes with Pecans

Ingredients

- 2 lbs sweet potatoes (cut to ½ inch slices and peeled)
- 1 cup apple juice (100%, unsweetened)
- 1 tablespoon ground cinnamon
- ½ teaspoon allspice
- ¼ teaspoon ground cloves
- Pecans (optional topping)
- Nutmeg and cinnamon for tasting
- Maple syrup or honey (if you prefer a sweeter version)

Directions

1. Prepare sweet potatoes and put inside your slow cooker. Add ½ cup of apple juice and spices.
2. Cook for about 4-5 hours on low heat until the potatoes are tender. Once potatoes are fully cooked, use hand blender to blend sweet potatoes inside the slow cooker. Add the remaining ½ cup of apple juice and blend well. Season more with nutmeg and cinnamon. Top with pecans if preferred.
3. Serve and enjoy!

Vegetarian Lasagna

Ingredients

- 1 26 oz jar of marinara sauce
- 1 14 ½ oz can of diced tomatoes
- 1 8 oz pack of no-boil lasagna noodles
- 1 15 oz container of part-skimmed ricotta cheese
- 1 8 oz pack of mozzarella (shredded)
- 1 10 oz pack of frozen spinach (thawed, chopped and squeezed to dry)
- 1 cup veggie crumbles (frozen)

Directions

1. In a medium-sized bowl, combine tomatoes with their juices and marinara sauce.
2. Meanwhile, using a non-stick cooking spray, spray the bottom of the Crock-Pot. Spoon a cup of tomato sauce mixture into the bottom.
3. Arrange ¼ of the noodles over the sauce. Overlap the noodles and make sure to break them in order to cover much of the sauce.
4. Spoon about ¾ cup of sauce on top of the noodles and top it with a half a cup of ricotta and half a cup of shredded mozzarella. Spread half of the spinach on top of the cheese.
5. Repeat doing the same process, twice beginning with the noodles. Once in the middle layer, replace the spinach using the frozen crumbles. Put remaining noodles and top it with the remaining sauce and cheese.
6. Cover and cook for about 2 ½ - 3 hours on low while 1 ½ - 2 hours on high or you can check to see if the noodles are already tender. Serve hot and enjoy!

Easy Southeast Asian Veggies

Ingredients

- 1 piece of butternut squash (around 2¾ lbs.; quartered, unpeeled and cut to 2-inch chunks)
- 4 pieces of sweet potatoes (peeled and cut to 2-inch chunks)
- 10 oz shiitake mushrooms (halved and stemmed)
- A bunch of scallions (separate the white and green parts; cut to an inch pieces)
- 2 14 oz cans of coconut milk
- 1 ½ cups water
- 3 tablespoons soy sauce
- 2 teaspoons sambal olek (you can also use other chili paste)
- 1 teaspoon Kosher salt
- 1 cup cilantro leaves (chopped roughly for garnish)
- ¼ cup salted peanuts (chopped roughly for garnish)

Directions

1. Place squash, shiitakes, scallions (white part only) and potatoes inside the Crock-Pot.
2. In a separate bowl, whisk coconut, water, milk, soy sauce, salt and sambal. Pour inside the Crock-Pot with the veggies then cover.
3. Cook for 4 hours on high or until veggies become tender.

4. Ladle on serving bowls and top with green scallions, peanuts, and scallions. Serve and enjoy!

Hearty Seafood and Fish Chowder

Ingredients

- 4 slices of chopped bacon
- 1 chopped onion
- 2 cloves of minced garlic
- 6 cups of chicken stock
- 1 cup of corn kernels (fresh)
- 2 large sized potatoes (diced)
- 3 stalks of diced celery
- 2 large sized carrots (diced)
- Black pepper (ground)
- ½ teaspoon red pepper flakes
- 1 cup of scallops
- 1 cup of medium-sized uncooked shrimp (deveined and peeled)
- ¼ lbs of halibut (cut to bite size pieces)
- 1 12 oz can of evaporated milk

Directions

1. Cook bacon for about 5-8 minutes over medium-high heat until it is browned. Drain excess oil. Add garlic and onion to the bacon and sauté around 5 minutes or until onion becomes translucent and garlic becomes fragrant. Transfer to the Crock-Pot cooker.
2. Pour the chicken stock, then add potatoes, corn, carrots, and celery. Season with red pepper flakes and black pepper. Cook for about 3 hours on high.
3. Once done, stir in the shrimp, halibut and scallops and cook for another hour. Stir in evaporated milk until heated through.
4. Ladle on serving bowls. Serve hot and enjoy!

Chapter 7 – Sweet Endings

A great meal would definitely be not complete without a perfect ending and this chapter will provide you great recipes to end your perfect meal! Who would have thought that the Crock-Pot can also give us great desserts? Go ahead and check them out!

Cranberry and Apple Dump Cake

Ingredients

- 4 cups of medium-sized apples (sliced)
- 1 cup of cranberries (you can use frozen or fresh)
- 1 teaspoon of vanilla
- ½ cup of brown sugar (light colored)
- 2 teaspoons of cinnamon (ground)
- 1 box of yellow cake mix (you can choose the brand you prefer)
- ½ cup of melted butter
- Whipped cream (optional)

Directions

1. Grease your Crock-Pot cooker with butter. You can also use cooking spray if you like.
2. Add the sliced apples, vanilla, cranberries, brown sugar and a teaspoon of cinnamon inside the Crock-Pot cooker. Toss and combine well.
3. Meanwhile, using a separate bowl, mix the dry cake mix plus the remaining teaspoon of cinnamon. Add them on top of the fruit mix inside the Crock-Pot cooker and drizzle it with melted butter.
4. Cover and cook for 3 hours on high setting or until you can see that the fruit is already bubbling on its edges.
5. Serve warm topped with whipped cream if you want. Enjoy!

Peach Cobbler

Ingredients

- 6 oz brown sugar (dark)
- 3 ½ oz rolled oats
- 4 oz all-purpose flour
- ½ teaspoon baking powder
- ½ teaspoon ground allspice
- ½ teaspoon grated nutmeg
- ¼ teaspoon Kosher salt
- ¼ cup unsalted butter (melted at room temperature plus additional for Crock-Pot cooker)
- 20 oz peach slices (frozen)

Directions

1. Combine oats, sugar, flour, baking powder, nutmeg, salt, and allspice in a big bowl. Add butter and gently combine well until the texture becomes crumbly. Fold in the slices of peach.
2. Meanwhile, butter the surface of the Crock-Pot including the sides. Add mixture inside and cook for about 3-3 ½ hours on low.
3. Serve immediately and enjoy!

Gooey Chocolatey Brownie Cake

Ingredients

- 1 ½ sticks of unsalted butter (melted and additional more for greasing)
- 1 ½ cups sugar
- 2/3 cups cocoa powder (unsweetened)
- 1/3 cup all-purpose flour
- 3 large eggs (beat lightly)
- 1 teaspoon vanilla extract (pure)
- Kosher salt
- ½ cup of chunks of semisweet chocolate
- Vanilla ice cream to serve

Directions

1. Line the bottom of the Crock-Pot with a piece of large foil then grease it generously with butter.
2. Using a bowl, whisk sugar, melted butter, cocoa powder, eggs, flour, ½ teaspoon of salt, and vanilla. Fold in the chocolate then scrape the batter to the lined foil inside the Crock-Pot. Make sure to spread it evenly then cover.
3. Cook for about 3 hours on low. Cake should be gooey in its center while the edges are already set.
4. Serve cake warm and top it with vanilla ice cream if desired. Enjoy!

Upside Down Banana Cake

Ingredients

For the banana:

- 5 tablespoons butter (unsalted plus additional for the cooker)
- ¾ cup brown sugar (dark; plus additional for the cooker)
- 3 tablespoons dark rum
- 2 lbs ripe, medium-sized bananas (peeled and sliced lengthwise)

For the cake:

- ¾ cup cake flour
- ¾ teaspoon baking powder
- ½ teaspoon cinnamon (ground)
- ¼ teaspoon nutmeg (ground)
- ¼ teaspoon fine salt
- 4 tablespoons of butter (unsalted; softened)
- 2/3 cups sugar
- 1 large egg (room temperature)
- 1 large egg yolk (room temperature)
- 2 tablespoons whole milk (room temperature)
- Ice cream to serve

Directions

1. To prepare the bananas: butter the insides of the Crock-Pot and line it completely with aluminum foil. Butter the foil too. Turn Crock-Pot to high and sprinkle lined foil with brown sugar, butter and rum. Cover it with the sliced bananas and press the bananas into the brown sugar.

2. To prepare the cake: sift baking powder, flour, nutmeg, cinnamon and salt using a large sized bowl. Whisk to combine well.

3. Using another bowl, beat sugar and butter lightly using an electric mixer until fully combined. Raise speed to high and continue beating mixture around 10 minutes until it becomes fluffy and light. Scrape the sides occasionally. Add the egg and yolk and continue to beat until it is fully incorporated in the mixture.

4. While beating it slowly, add flour mixture in three parts into the butter. Alternate it with milk in two parts making sure that the beginning and the ending will be the flour mixture. Mix well on medium speed until the batter becomes smooth.

5. Pour this batter over the bananas inside the Crock-Pot then evenly smooth it out using your spatula. Place a paper towel on top of the Crock-Pot. Make sure that it is covered well to seal it tightly because Crock-Pot cooks with moisture. The paper towel will help collecting excess moisture and avoid it from dripping down the cake.

6. Cover lid tightly and continue cooking around 3 ½ hours on high setting until cake starts browning slightly on its sides and springs back when you touch the middle of the cake. Turn off the cooker and let cake set. Wait for about 20 more minutes.

7. Lift cake using the sides of the aluminum foil and set aside. Let cook for about 30 minutes. Invert the cake carefully on the platter making sure that caramelized bananas will be the ones facing you.

8. Spoon or slice the cakes and place on serving bowls. If you want, you can top it with your favorite plain ice cream. Enjoy!

Conclusion

Congratulations! You have reached the end of this recipe book. I hope that you have enjoyed preparing all the delicious and mouth-watering dishes inside. Cooking is such a work of art. We all continue to discover useful and helpful innovations in our everyday food preparation and the Crock-Pot is of great help in letting us prepare unique meals for the whole family. Who doesn't want to give the best food to their loved ones, right?

If you haven't tried all of the recipes yet, make sure that you do! Share them with your friends and family. Involve your kids while preparing these meals and show them the magic of the Crock-Pot cooker.

Finally, if you liked the book, please leave a word or two at Amazon.com. Your feedback will be highly appreciated.

Have fun and enjoy cooking! Bon appétit!

-- Debbie Butler

www.ingramcontent.com/pod-product-compliance
Lightning Source LLC
LaVergne TN
LVHW061652090125
800915LV00004B/26